ARIZONA CARDINALS

ELLIOTT SMITH

WWW.APEXEDITIONS.COM

Copyright © 2025 by Apex Editions, Mendota Heights, MN 55120. All rights reserved. No part of this book may be reproduced or utilized in any form or by any means without written permission from the publisher.

Apex is distributed by North Star Editions:
sales@northstareditions.com | 888-417-0195

Produced for Apex by Red Line Editorial.

Photographs ©: Kamil Krzaczynski/AP Images, cover, 1; Shutterstock Images, 4–5; Norm Hall/Getty Images Sport/Getty Images, 6–7, 44–45; Bettmann/Getty Images, 8–9, 12–13; Pro Football Hall of Fame/AP Images, 10–11; Focus On Sport/Getty Images Sport/Getty Images, 14–15, 24–25, 26–27; Stephen Dunn/Allsport/Getty Images Sport/Getty Images, 16–17; Four Seam Images/AP Images, 19; AP Images, 20–21; Tony Tomsic/AP Images, 22–23, 58–59; Marco Ugargte/AP Images, 28–29; Chris Graythen/Getty Images Sport/Getty Images, 30–31; Greg Trott/AP Images, 32–33; Jared C. Tilton/Getty Images Sport/Getty Images, 34–35; Kevin Terrell/AP Images, 37; Bernie Nunez/Getty Images Sport/Getty Images, 38–39; Robert B. Stanton/NFLPhotoLibrary/Getty Images Sport/Getty Images, 40–41; Gene Lower/Getty Images Sport/Getty Images, 42–43; Paul Connors/AP Images, 47, 57; Sean M. Haffey/Getty Images Sport/Getty Images, 48–49; Christian Petersen/Getty Images Sport/Getty Images, 50–51; Kirby Lee/AP Images, 52–53; Gene Lower/AP Images, 54–55

Library of Congress Control Number: 2023921773

ISBN
979-8-89250-147-7 (hardcover)
979-8-89250-164-4 (paperback)
979-8-89250-288-7 (ebook pdf)
979-8-89250-181-1 (hosted ebook)

Printed in the United States of America
Mankato, MN
012025

NOTE TO PARENTS AND EDUCATORS
Apex books are designed to build literacy skills in striving readers. Exciting, high-interest content attracts and holds readers' attention. The text is carefully leveled to allow students to achieve success quickly.

TABLE OF CONTENTS

CHAPTER 1
BIRD GANG 4

CHAPTER 2
EARLY HISTORY 8

PLAYER SPOTLIGHT
LARRY WILSON 18

CHAPTER 3
LEGENDS 20

CHAPTER 4
RECENT HISTORY 28

PLAYER SPOTLIGHT
PAT TILLMAN 36

CHAPTER 5
MODERN STARS 38

PLAYER SPOTLIGHT
LARRY FITZGERALD 46

CHAPTER 6
TEAM TRIVIA 48

TEAM RECORDS • 56
TIMELINE • 58
COMPREHENSION QUESTIONS • 60
GLOSSARY • 62
TO LEARN MORE • 63
ABOUT THE AUTHOR • 63

CHAPTER 1

BIRD GANG

A sea of red fills the stadium. The fans rise to their feet. They cheer for the Arizona Cardinals. Quarterback Kyler Murray takes the snap. He is one of the NFL's fastest players. Murray looks for a receiver. But then he decides to run. He scores a touchdown. The crowd goes wild.

Kyler Murray ran for 26 touchdowns in his first five seasons.

Running back James Conner sports Arizona's black uniform during a 2023 game against the Cincinnati Bengals.

The Cardinals are the oldest team in the NFL. They have a long history on the field. They also have a loyal fan base. Cardinals fans are known as the Bird Gang.

CARDINAL BLACK

The Cardinals are famous for their red jerseys. But they also have an alternate uniform. Sometimes the team wears black. Arizona introduced the black jerseys in 2010.

CHAPTER 2

EARLY HISTORY

The Arizona Cardinals trace their history to 1898. A group of friends began playing football in Chicago, Illinois. They were called the Morgan Athletic Club. A few years later, the team's owner bought some old jerseys. The shirts were cardinal red. The team's nickname was born.

The Chicago Cardinals take on the Chicago Bears in the 1920s.

Fullback Ernie Nevers was one of the Cardinals' top players in the team's early days.

The NFL formed in 1920. The Cardinals joined the new league. The team played at Normal Park. It was on Chicago's South Side. In 1922, the Cardinals started playing at Comiskey Park. They shared the stadium with baseball's Chicago White Sox.

FAMILY TIES

In 1932, Charles Bidwill bought the Cardinals. Bidwill died in 1947. His wife, Violet, became the NFL's first female owner. The Bidwill family still owns the Cardinals today.

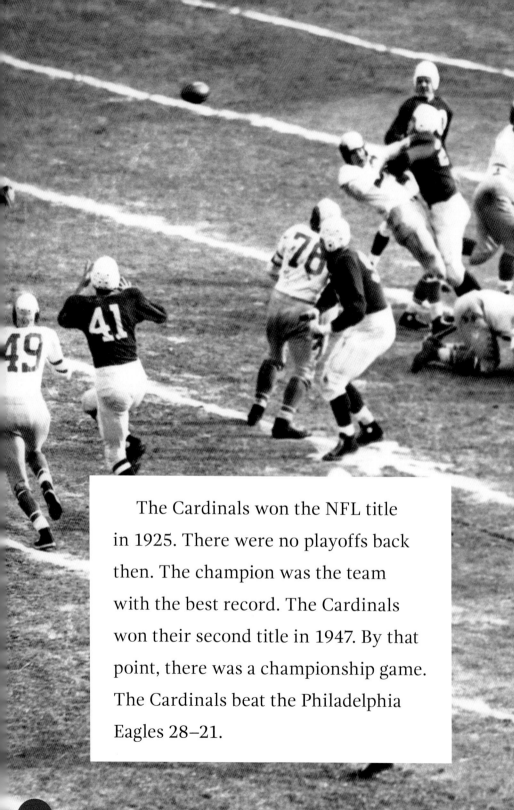

The Cardinals won the NFL title in 1925. There were no playoffs back then. The champion was the team with the best record. The Cardinals won their second title in 1947. By that point, there was a championship game. The Cardinals beat the Philadelphia Eagles 28–21.

WAR SQUAD

Many pro football players fought in World War II (1939–1945). That left some teams short of players. In 1944, the Cardinals joined the Pittsburgh Steelers. They were known as Card-Pitt. The team finished the season 0–10.

The Cardinals take on the Eagles at Comiskey Park in the 1947 title game.

The Cardinals made the championship game again in 1948. But after that, the team struggled. Most fans in Chicago started cheering for the Bears. So, in 1960, the Cardinals moved to St. Louis, Missouri.

The Cardinals rarely reached the playoffs in their new city. And when they did, they couldn't find a way to win. Once again, fans started losing interest.

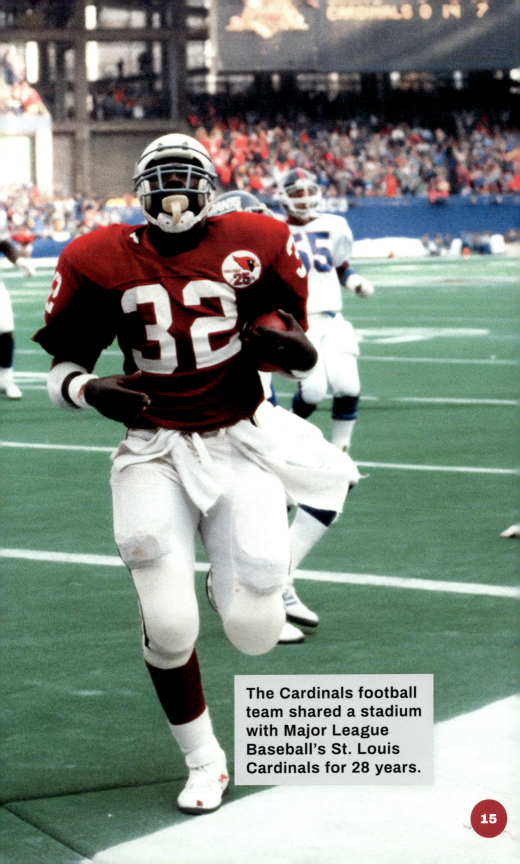

The Cardinals football team shared a stadium with Major League Baseball's St. Louis Cardinals for 28 years.

In 1988, the team moved again. This time, the Cardinals went to Arizona. In 1998, the team finally ended its 15-year playoff drought. Arizona played the Dallas Cowboys in the first round. Most people expected Dallas to win. But the Cardinals came out on top. It was the team's first playoff win since 1947.

HOT STUFF

The Cardinals spent 18 seasons at Sun Devil Stadium. It was outdoors. Games could get very hot. The Cardinals usually wore white. Visiting teams had to wear darker jerseys. Those could get hot in the sun.

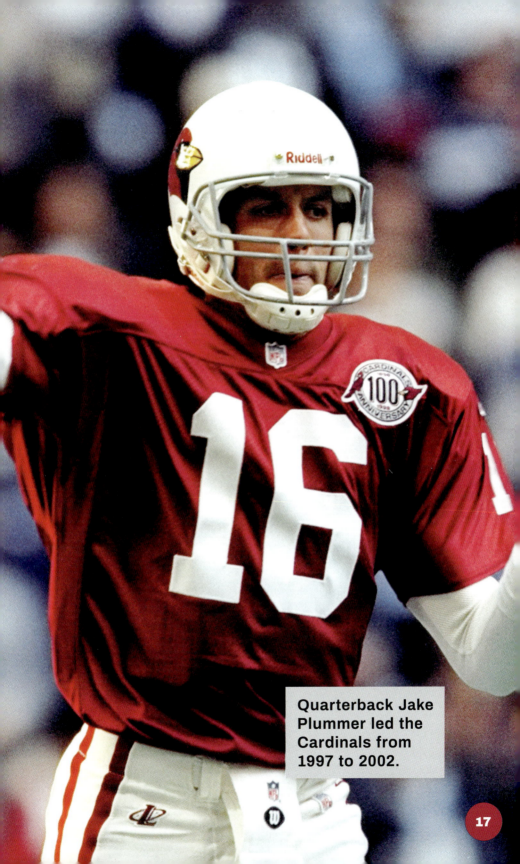

Quarterback Jake Plummer led the Cardinals from 1997 to 2002.

PLAYER SPOTLIGHT

LARRY WILSON

Larry Wilson went from long shot to superstar. The safety joined the Cardinals in 1960. He wasn't very tall. So, most teams didn't expect him to succeed. But the Cardinals took a chance on him. Wilson went on to have a Hall of Fame career.

Wilson was one of the first safeties to rush the quarterback. He was also great at covering receivers. Wilson pulled down 52 interceptions in his 13-year career. After retiring, he spent 30 years working in the team's front office.

LARRY WILSON MADE THE PRO BOWL EIGHT TIMES DURING HIS CAREER.

CHAPTER 3
LEGENDS

Many talented players have taken the field for the Cardinals. Dick "Night Train" Lane was one of the best cornerbacks of all time. He was traded to the Cardinals in 1954. That year, he intercepted 10 passes. In his six seasons with the team, Lane racked up 30 interceptions.

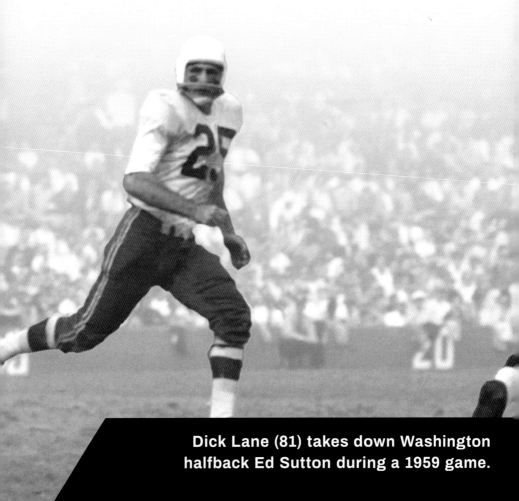

Dick Lane (81) takes down Washington halfback Ed Sutton during a 1959 game.

Jackie Smith helped change the tight end position. In football's early days, tight ends mostly blocked. But Smith caught more than 40 passes in seven different seasons. He also served as the Cardinals' punter for three seasons.

GOOD FOOT

Kicker Jim Bakken spent 17 seasons with the Cardinals. He became the team's all-time leading scorer. Bakken also played in 234 games with the Cardinals. That was a team record for more than 40 years.

Jackie Smith dives for extra yards during a game against the Dallas Cowboys.

Jim Hart (17) threw 209 touchdown passes during his long career with the Cardinals.

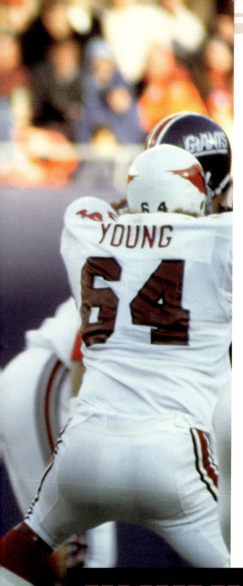

Quarterback Jim Hart played 18 seasons with the Cardinals. He is the team's all-time leader in passing yards and touchdown passes. Hart was also the leader of the "Cardiac Cards." He helped the team win many close games in the 1970s.

TOO GOOD TO IGNORE

Offensive linemen don't get much glory. But Dan Dierdorf was no ordinary lineman. Fans had to take notice of his speed and strength. Dierdorf was great at both pass blocking and run blocking. He made the Pro Bowl six times in his 13-year career.

In the 1979 draft, the Cardinals used their top pick on Ottis Anderson. The running back made an impact right away. Anderson ran for 193 yards in his first NFL game. He won the Rookie of the Year Award that season. Anderson piled up at least 1,000 yards in five different seasons.

AIR CORYELL

Don Coryell became the Cardinals' head coach in 1973. The next year, he took the team to the playoffs. Coryell was known for calling many passing plays. That's how he earned the name "Air Coryell."

Ottis Anderson ran for 7,999 yards as a member of the Cardinals.

CHAPTER 4

RECENT HISTORY

The Cardinals struggled after their 1998 playoff appearance. But the team still made history. In 2005, the Cardinals took part in the NFL's first game outside the United States. It was in Mexico City. Arizona beat the San Francisco 49ers 31–14.

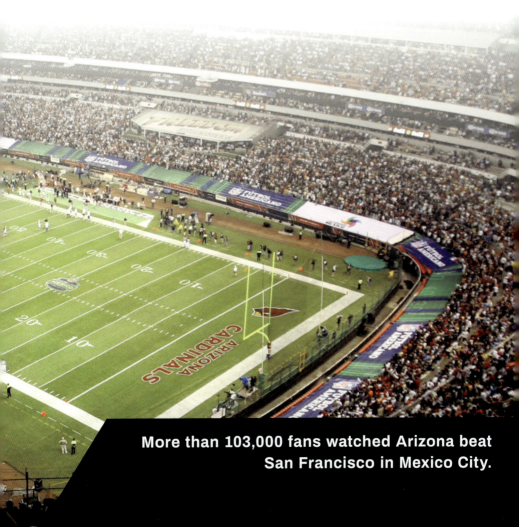

More than 103,000 fans watched Arizona beat San Francisco in Mexico City.

Wide receiver Ben Patrick (89) hauls in a touchdown catch in the Super Bowl.

Arizona had a season to remember in 2008. The Cardinals reached the Super Bowl for the first time. In that game, Arizona took the lead in the fourth quarter. But the Pittsburgh Steelers came back to win 27–23. It was a tough loss for Cardinals fans.

HOME SWEET HOME

In 2006, the Cardinals moved into a new stadium. It marked the first time the Cardinals didn't have to share their stadium with another team. The new stadium has hosted the Super Bowl three times.

The Cardinals went 10–6 in 2009. It was their best record since moving to Arizona. Then they treated fans to a thrilling playoff game. Arizona faced the Green Bay Packers. The game went back and forth. Green Bay scored a late touchdown to tie the game. But the Cardinals pulled out a 51–45 win in overtime.

Larry Fitzgerald (11) scored two touchdowns in Arizona's playoff win over Green Bay.

David Johnson (31) pounds the ball into the end zone during the conference championship game.

Starting in 2013, the Cardinals put together three straight winning seasons. In 2015, Arizona won 13 games. That was the most in team history. The Cardinals made it to the conference championship game. But they couldn't stop the Carolina Panthers. Arizona lost 49–15.

COACH A

Bruce Arians became the Cardinals' head coach in 2013. He spent five years with Arizona. In that time, he won 49 games. That was the most coaching wins in team history.

PLAYER SPOTLIGHT

PAT TILLMAN

Pat Tillman was a hard-hitting safety. In the 2000 season, he recorded 155 tackles. Tillman was a star on the rise. Arizona wanted to give him a big contract. But in 2002, Tillman walked away from football. He joined the US Army. In 2003, Tillman served in Iraq. The next year, he served in Afghanistan. While there, Tillman was killed.

In 2006, the Cardinals honored Tillman. They added him to their Ring of Honor. The team also built a statue of him. It stands outside the Cardinals' stadium.

PAT TILLMAN RECORDED 374 TACKLES DURING HIS NFL CAREER.

CHAPTER 5

MODERN STARS

Aeneas Williams was a great cornerback for the Cardinals. The team drafted him in 1991. He spent 10 seasons with Arizona. In that time, Williams had 46 interceptions. He ran six of them back for touchdowns.

In 2014, Aeneas Williams earned a spot in the Pro Football Hall of Fame.

Kurt Warner won a Super Bowl with the St. Louis Rams in the 1999 season. He signed with Arizona in 2005. Three years later, he had one of the best seasons of his career. Warner tossed 30 touchdown passes. He also led the Cardinals to their first Super Bowl.

STAR RUNNERS

Two great running backs played for the Cardinals in the 2000s. Both were near the end of their careers. Emmitt Smith spent two seasons with Arizona. Edgerrin James spent three seasons with the team.

Kurt Warner was the second quarterback in history to lead two teams to the Super Bowl.

Adrian Wilson returns an interception during a 2008 game against the San Francisco 49ers.

Adrian Wilson played his entire career with the Cardinals. The defensive back was drafted in 2001. He made the Pro Bowl five times in 12 years. Wilson had a huge season in 2005. He recorded 109 tackles. He also had eight sacks and two fumble recoveries.

Kyler Murray (1) earned his first Pro Bowl nod in the 2020 season.

Kyler Murray was the first pick in the 2019 NFL Draft. The young quarterback had a great arm. He was also an excellent runner. Both skills were on display in the 2020 season. Murray threw 26 touchdown passes. He ran for 11 more. In 2021, he led Arizona to the playoffs.

TOUCHDOWN TIME

James Conner went touchdown crazy in 2021. The running back reached the end zone 18 times. Three of those scores were receiving touchdowns. The other 15 were runs.

PLAYER SPOTLIGHT

LARRY FITZGERALD

Arizona drafted Larry Fitzgerald in 2004. The wide receiver spent his entire 17-year career with the Cardinals. During that time, Fitzgerald set dozens of team records. For example, he had 17,492 career receiving yards. That was the second-most of any player in NFL history.

In 2019, the NFL marked its 100th year. The league made a list of the all-time best players at each position. Not surprisingly, Fitzgerald was included on the list.

LARRY FITZGERALD SCORED 121 TOUCHDOWNS DURING HIS CAREER.

CHAPTER 6

TEAM TRIVIA

Arizona's biggest rival is the Los Angeles Rams. The teams first played each other in 1937. Since then, they have met more than 90 times. Strangely, both teams have been based in St. Louis. The Cardinals called the city home from 1960 to 1987. The Rams were there from 1995 to 2015.

Wide receiver Rondale Moore makes a move during a 2022 game against the Los Angeles Rams.

The Cardinals' mascot is named Big Red. He is one of the best-known mascots in the NFL. The Cardinals claim that Big Red hatched in 1998. That was 10 years after the team moved to Arizona.

SLOW START
The Cardinals' first NFL game took place in 1920. They played the Chicago Tigers. Fans didn't see much offense. The game ended in a 0–0 tie.

Big Red fires up the crowd at Cardinals home games.

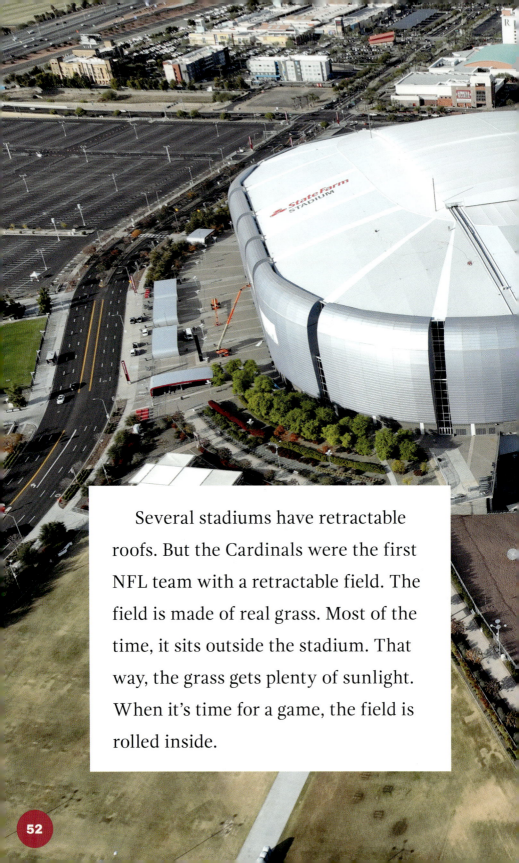

Several stadiums have retractable roofs. But the Cardinals were the first NFL team with a retractable field. The field is made of real grass. Most of the time, it sits outside the stadium. That way, the grass gets plenty of sunlight. When it's time for a game, the field is rolled inside.

It takes about 70 minutes to roll the field into or out of the stadium.

Spanish-language announcers Gabriel Trujillo and Rolando Cantu helped bring Cardinals games to a wider audience.

Many people in Arizona speak Spanish. And the state shares a border with Mexico. In 2000, the Cardinals started broadcasting all their games in Spanish. They were the first NFL team to do that. Cardinals games can also be heard on the radio in cities throughout Mexico.

THE VOICE

Blake Shelton is a well-known country singer. He is also one of the Cardinals' most famous fans. Shelton even has a Cardinals room in his house. The room is filled with team memorabilia and photos.

TEAM RECORDS

All-Time Passing Yards: 34,639
  Jim Hart (1966–83)

All-Time Touchdown Passes: 209
  Jim Hart (1966–83)

All-Time Rushing Yards: 7,999
  Ottis Anderson (1979–86)

All-Time Receiving Yards: 17,492
  Larry Fitzgerald (2004–20)

All-Time Receiving Touchdowns: 121
  Larry Fitzgerald (2004–20)

All-Time Interceptions: 52
  Larry Wilson (1960–72)

All-Time Sacks: 71.5
  Chandler Jones (2016–21)

All-Time Scoring: 1,380
  Jim Bakken (1962–78)

All-Time Coaching Wins: 49
  Bruce Arians (2013–17)

NFL Titles: 2
  (1925, 1947)

All statistics are accurate through 2023.

TIMELINE

1898

1901

1920

1925

1944

Neighborhood friends in Chicago form the Morgan Athletic Club.

The team changes its name to the Racine Street Cardinals.

The Cardinals join the newly formed NFL.

The Cardinals win their first NFL title.

During World War II, the Cardinals join with the Pittsburgh Steelers to form Card-Pitt.

1947 — The Chicago Cardinals defeat the Philadelphia Eagles to win their second NFL title.

1960 — The Cardinals move to St. Louis, Missouri.

1988 — The team moves to Arizona and becomes the Phoenix Cardinals. Six years later, the team changes its name to the Arizona Cardinals.

1998 — The Cardinals make the playoffs for the first time in 16 years and win their first playoff game since 1947.

2008 — The Cardinals reach the Super Bowl for the first time in team history.

COMPREHENSION QUESTIONS

Write your answers on a separate piece of paper.

1. Write a paragraph that explains the main ideas of Chapter 2.

2. What do you think is the most important moment in Cardinals history? Why?

3. Which team did the Cardinals beat in Mexico City in 2005?

    A. Green Bay Packers

    B. San Francisco 49ers

    C. Dallas Cowboys

4. How did the Cardinals get their name?

    A. The team's first owner loved bird-watching.

    B. The team's first owner bought red jerseys.

    C. The team's first owner asked fans to vote for a name.

5. What does **drought** mean in this book?

*In 1998, the team finally ended its 15-year playoff **drought**. Arizona played the Dallas Cowboys in the first round. Most people expected Dallas to win. But the Cardinals came out on top.*

- **A.** a play that helps a team win the game
- **B.** a series of games to decide the champion
- **C.** a long period without success

6. What does **rival** mean in this book?

*Arizona's biggest **rival** is the Los Angeles Rams. The teams first played each other in 1937. Since then, they have met more than 90 times.*

- **A.** a team that brings out strong emotions from fans and players
- **B.** a game between two teams that don't face each other very often
- **C.** a win that helps a team earn a spot in the playoffs

Answer key on page 64.

GLOSSARY

broadcasting
Sending out radio or TV signals.

conference
A group of teams that make up part of a sports league.

contract
An agreement to pay someone money, often for doing work.

draft
A system that lets teams select new players coming into the league.

front office
The workers who deal with the business side of a sports team.

mascot
A figure that is the symbol of a sports team. It is often a person in a costume.

memorabilia
Objects kept or collected because of their historical interest.

playoffs
A set of games played after the regular season to decide which team is the champion.

retractable
Able to move back and forth.

rookie
An athlete in his or her first year as a professional player.

TO LEARN MORE

BOOKS

Coleman, Ted. *Arizona Cardinals All-Time Greats*. Mendota Heights, MN: Press Box Books, 2022.

Olson, Ethan. *Great NFL Super Bowl Championships*. San Diego: BrightPoint Press, 2024.

Scheffer, Janie. *Arizona Cardinals*. Minneapolis: Bellwether Media, 2024.

ONLINE RESOURCES

Visit **www.apexeditions.com** to find links and resources related to this title.

ABOUT THE AUTHOR

Elliott Smith is a writer who lives just outside Washington, DC, with his wife and two children. He used to be a sports reporter, and he covered athletes from high school to the pros. He loves reading, watching sports on TV and in person, going to concerts, and collecting sports jerseys.

INDEX

Anderson, Ottis, 26
Arians, Bruce, 35

Bakken, Jim, 22
Bidwill, Charles, 11
Bidwill, Violet, 11

Card-Pitt, 13
Conner, James, 45
Coryell, Don, 26

Dierdorf, Dan, 25

Fitzgerald, Larry, 46

Hart, Jim, 25

James, Edgerrin, 40

Lane, Dick, 21

mascot, 50
Morgan Athletic Club, 9

Murray, Kyler, 4, 45

rivals, 48

Shelton, Blake, 55
Smith, Emmitt, 40
Smith, Jackie, 22
stadium, 4, 11, 16, 31, 36, 52
Sun Devil Stadium, 16
Super Bowl, 31, 40

Tillman, Pat, 36

Warner, Kurt, 40
Williams, Aeneas, 38
Wilson, Adrian, 43
Wilson, Larry, 18

ANSWER KEY:
1. Answers will vary; 2. Answers will vary; 3. B; 4. B; 5. C; 6. A